50 Big Book of Cold Brew Coffee Recipes

By: Kelly Johnson

Table of Contents

- Classic Cold Brew Coffee
- Vanilla Bean Cold Brew Latte
- Iced Cold Brew with Almond Milk
- Cold Brew Mocha
- Cinnamon Cold Brew Coffee
- Cold Brew Coffee Smoothie
- Nitro Cold Brew
- Coconut Milk Cold Brew Latte
- Cold Brew with Hazelnut Syrup
- Salted Caramel Cold Brew
- Iced Cold Brew Coffee Float
- Cold Brew Coffee with Sweetened Condensed Milk
- Pumpkin Spice Cold Brew
- Cold Brew Coffee with Oat Milk
- Irish Cream Cold Brew
- Chocolate Mint Cold Brew
- Cold Brew Affogato
- Coconut Cream Cold Brew Latte
- Cold Brew Coffee with Cold Foam
- Cold Brew and Lemonade
- Cold Brew Iced Coffee with Cinnamon and Honey
- Cold Brew with Vanilla Almond Milk
- Brown Sugar Cinnamon Cold Brew
- Cold Brew Coffee with Maple Syrup
- Caramelized Banana Cold Brew Smoothie
- Mocha Almond Cold Brew
- Cold Brew Coffee with Coconut Water
- Cold Brew Coffee Mojito
- Iced Nitro Cold Brew Float
- Cold Brew Coffee with Cardamom
- Honey Lavender Cold Brew
- Cold Brew Ginger Coffee
- Cold Brew Frappe
- Matcha Cold Brew Latte
- Cold Brew with Chocolate Syrup

- Strawberry Cold Brew Iced Coffee
- Spiced Pumpkin Cold Brew Latte
- Cold Brew Coffee Milkshake
- Cold Brew Coffee with Coconut Milk and Spice
- Cold Brew Cherry Blossom Latte
- Cold Brew Coffee with Vanilla Syrup
- Cold Brew Coffee Tonic
- Lemon Ginger Cold Brew Coffee
- Cold Brew Coconut Iced Coffee
- Cherry Cold Brew Coffee
- Cold Brew Caramel Macchiato
- Cold Brew Coffee with Coconut Cream and Cocoa
- Tropical Cold Brew Coffee
- Cold Brew Coffee with Orange Zest
- Cold Brew Coffee with Almond Syrup

Classic Cold Brew Coffee

Ingredients:

- 1 cup coarsely ground coffee
- 4 cups cold water

Instructions:

1. **Prepare the Coffee**: In a large jar or pitcher, combine the ground coffee and cold water. Stir well to ensure all the coffee grounds are wet.
2. **Steep**: Cover and let the coffee steep in the refrigerator for 12-24 hours.
3. **Strain**: After steeping, strain the coffee through a fine mesh sieve or coffee filter to remove the grounds.
4. **Serve**: Pour the cold brew concentrate over ice and enjoy as is, or dilute with water or milk if desired.

Vanilla Bean Cold Brew Latte

Ingredients:

- 1 cup cold brew coffee
- 1/2 cup milk or dairy alternative
- 1 tbsp vanilla syrup or vanilla extract
- Ice

   Instructions:
1. **Mix the Ingredients**: In a glass, combine the cold brew coffee, milk, and vanilla syrup or extract. Stir to combine.
2. **Serve**: Add ice to a glass and pour the mixture over. Stir and serve chilled.

Iced Cold Brew with Almond Milk

Ingredients:

- 1 cup cold brew coffee
- 1/2 cup almond milk (or preferred milk)
- Ice
- Sweetener (optional)

Instructions:

1. **Prepare the Drink**: In a glass, combine the cold brew coffee and almond milk. Add sweetener if desired and stir.
2. **Serve**: Fill a glass with ice and pour the mixture over. Stir to chill and enjoy.

Cold Brew Mocha

Ingredients:

- 1 cup cold brew coffee
- 1/4 cup chocolate syrup
- 1/2 cup milk or dairy alternative
- Ice

    Instructions:

1. **Mix the Ingredients**: In a glass, combine cold brew coffee, chocolate syrup, and milk. Stir until well mixed.
2. **Serve**: Add ice to a glass and pour the mixture over. Stir and enjoy.

Cinnamon Cold Brew Coffee

Ingredients:

- 1 cup cold brew coffee
- 1/2 tsp ground cinnamon
- 1 tbsp honey or sweetener of choice
- Ice

   Instructions:
1. **Mix the Ingredients**: In a glass, combine cold brew coffee, ground cinnamon, and honey. Stir until well combined.
2. **Serve**: Add ice to a glass and pour the mixture over. Stir and enjoy a spiced, refreshing cold brew.

Cold Brew Coffee Smoothie

Ingredients:

- 1 cup cold brew coffee
- 1/2 frozen banana
- 1/4 cup milk or dairy alternative
- 1 tbsp peanut butter or almond butter
- 1 tsp honey or sweetener (optional)
  Instructions:
1. **Blend the Ingredients**: In a blender, combine cold brew coffee, frozen banana, milk, peanut butter, and honey. Blend until smooth.
2. **Serve**: Pour into a glass and enjoy a creamy and energizing cold brew smoothie.

Nitro Cold Brew

Ingredients:

- 1 cup cold brew coffee
- Nitrogen-infused cold brew coffee (via a nitrogen dispenser or canned)

Instructions:

1. **Pour the Cold Brew**: Pour cold brew coffee into a glass.
2. **Infuse with Nitrogen**: Using a nitrogen dispenser or canned nitro cold brew, pour the infused coffee over your regular cold brew coffee.
3. **Serve**: Stir slightly and enjoy the smooth, creamy texture of nitro cold brew.

Coconut Milk Cold Brew Latte

Ingredients:

- 1 cup cold brew coffee
- 1/2 cup coconut milk
- 1 tbsp maple syrup or sweetener of choice
- Ice

Instructions:

1. **Mix the Ingredients**: In a glass, combine cold brew coffee, coconut milk, and maple syrup. Stir well to mix.
2. **Serve**: Fill a glass with ice and pour the mixture over. Stir and enjoy a tropical, creamy cold brew.

Cold Brew with Hazelnut Syrup

Ingredients:

- 1 cup cold brew coffee
- 2 tbsp hazelnut syrup
- Ice
- Milk or dairy alternative (optional)

Instructions:

1. **Prepare the Drink**: In a glass, combine cold brew coffee and hazelnut syrup. Stir well to combine.
2. **Serve**: Fill a glass with ice and pour the mixture over. Add milk or dairy alternative if desired. Stir and enjoy!

Salted Caramel Cold Brew

Ingredients:

- 1 cup cold brew coffee
- 2 tbsp salted caramel syrup
- Ice
- Milk or dairy alternative (optional)
  Instructions:
1. **Mix the Ingredients**: In a glass, combine cold brew coffee and salted caramel syrup. Stir to combine.
2. **Serve**: Add ice to a glass and pour the mixture over. Stir and add milk if desired. Enjoy the sweet and salty flavor combination!

Iced Cold Brew Coffee Float

Ingredients:

- 1 cup cold brew coffee
- 1 scoop vanilla ice cream
- Ice

Instructions:

1. **Prepare the Drink**: In a tall glass, add ice and pour the cold brew coffee over it.
2. **Top with Ice Cream**: Add a scoop of vanilla ice cream on top of the coffee.
3. **Serve**: Stir gently and enjoy the creamy, chilled coffee float.

Cold Brew Coffee with Sweetened Condensed Milk

Ingredients:

- 1 cup cold brew coffee
- 2 tbsp sweetened condensed milk
- Ice
   Instructions:
1. **Mix the Ingredients**: In a glass, combine cold brew coffee and sweetened condensed milk. Stir well to ensure it's smooth.
2. **Serve**: Add ice to a glass and pour the mixture over. Stir and enjoy the rich, sweet flavor.

Pumpkin Spice Cold Brew

Ingredients:

- 1 cup cold brew coffee
- 2 tbsp pumpkin spice syrup
- 1/4 tsp cinnamon
- Ice
- Milk or dairy alternative (optional)
  Instructions:
1. **Prepare the Drink**: In a glass, combine cold brew coffee, pumpkin spice syrup, and cinnamon. Stir well to combine.
2. **Serve**: Fill a glass with ice and pour the mixture over. Add milk if desired. Stir and enjoy the fall-inspired flavors.

Cold Brew Coffee with Oat Milk

Ingredients:

- 1 cup cold brew coffee
- 1/2 cup oat milk
- Ice
- Sweetener (optional)
  Instructions:
1. **Mix the Ingredients**: In a glass, combine cold brew coffee and oat milk. Stir well.
2. **Serve**: Add ice to a glass and pour the mixture over. Add sweetener if desired and stir to enjoy a smooth and creamy drink.

Irish Cream Cold Brew

Ingredients:

- 1 cup cold brew coffee
- 2 tbsp Irish cream syrup
- Ice
- Milk or cream (optional)
  Instructions:
1. **Mix the Ingredients**: In a glass, combine cold brew coffee and Irish cream syrup. Stir until well combined.
2. **Serve**: Add ice to a glass and pour the mixture over. Add milk or cream for extra richness. Stir and enjoy.

Chocolate Mint Cold Brew

Ingredients:

- 1 cup cold brew coffee
- 2 tbsp chocolate syrup
- 1 tbsp mint syrup or mint extract
- Ice
- Milk or dairy alternative (optional)

Instructions:

1. **Prepare the Drink**: In a glass, combine cold brew coffee, chocolate syrup, and mint syrup. Stir until smooth.
2. **Serve**: Add ice to a glass and pour the mixture over. Add milk if desired. Stir and enjoy the refreshing chocolate-mint flavor.

Cold Brew Affogato

Ingredients:

- 1 cup cold brew coffee
- 1 scoop vanilla ice cream

Instructions:

1. **Prepare the Drink**: In a glass, add a scoop of vanilla ice cream.
2. **Pour the Coffee**: Pour the cold brew coffee directly over the ice cream.
3. **Serve**: Stir slightly to combine, allowing the cold brew to melt the ice cream for a creamy, coffee-infused treat.

Coconut Cream Cold Brew Latte

Ingredients:

- 1 cup cold brew coffee
- 1/4 cup coconut cream
- Ice
- Sweetener (optional)
  Instructions:
1. **Mix the Ingredients**: In a glass, combine cold brew coffee and coconut cream. Stir well to combine.
2. **Serve**: Fill a glass with ice and pour the mixture over. Sweeten if desired and stir to enjoy a creamy, tropical flavor.

Cold Brew Coffee with Cold Foam

Ingredients:

- 1 cup cold brew coffee
- 1/4 cup milk (or dairy-free alternative)
- 1 tbsp sweetener (optional)
- Ice

Instructions:

1. **Prepare the Cold Foam**: In a small jar, combine milk and sweetener, then shake vigorously to create foam.
2. **Serve**: Fill a glass with ice and pour cold brew coffee over. Spoon the cold foam on top and enjoy a smooth, creamy cold brew.

Cold Brew and Lemonade

Ingredients:

- 1/2 cup cold brew coffee
- 1/2 cup lemonade
- Ice

   Instructions:
1. **Combine the Drinks**: In a glass, mix cold brew coffee and lemonade.
2. **Serve**: Add ice to the glass and stir to combine. The result is a refreshing blend of coffee and citrus.

Cold Brew Iced Coffee with Cinnamon and Honey

Ingredients:

- 1 cup cold brew coffee
- 1/2 tsp cinnamon
- 1 tbsp honey
- Ice

    Instructions:
1. **Mix the Ingredients**: In a glass, combine cold brew coffee, cinnamon, and honey. Stir well until the honey is dissolved.
2. **Serve**: Add ice and stir again to enjoy a spiced, sweet iced coffee treat.

Cold Brew with Vanilla Almond Milk

Ingredients:

- 1 cup cold brew coffee
- 1/2 cup vanilla almond milk
- Ice
  Instructions:
1. **Mix the Ingredients**: In a glass, combine cold brew coffee and vanilla almond milk. Stir well.
2. **Serve**: Add ice to the glass and stir to enjoy a smooth, lightly sweetened coffee drink.

Brown Sugar Cinnamon Cold Brew

Ingredients:

- 1 cup cold brew coffee
- 2 tbsp brown sugar
- 1/2 tsp cinnamon
- Ice

    Instructions:

1. **Mix the Ingredients**: In a glass, combine cold brew coffee, brown sugar, and cinnamon. Stir well until the sugar is dissolved.
2. **Serve**: Add ice and stir again to enjoy the warm, spiced flavor.

Cold Brew Coffee with Maple Syrup

Ingredients:

- 1 cup cold brew coffee
- 2 tbsp maple syrup
- Ice
    Instructions:
1. **Mix the Ingredients**: In a glass, combine cold brew coffee and maple syrup. Stir well until smooth.
2. **Serve**: Add ice to the glass and stir to enjoy a subtly sweet and rich cold brew.

Caramelized Banana Cold Brew Smoothie

Ingredients:

- 1 ripe banana
- 1/2 cup cold brew coffee
- 1/4 cup milk (or dairy-free alternative)
- 1 tbsp caramel syrup
- Ice

Instructions:

1. **Caramelize the Banana**: In a pan, cook sliced banana over medium heat with a bit of caramel syrup until golden and softened.
2. **Blend**: In a blender, combine the caramelized banana, cold brew coffee, milk, and ice. Blend until smooth.
3. **Serve**: Pour into a glass and drizzle with extra caramel syrup if desired. Enjoy a creamy, coffee-infused smoothie.

Mocha Almond Cold Brew

Ingredients:

- 1 cup cold brew coffee
- 2 tbsp chocolate syrup
- 1 tbsp almond syrup
- Ice
- Whipped cream (optional)

Instructions:

1. **Mix the Ingredients**: In a glass, combine cold brew coffee, chocolate syrup, and almond syrup. Stir well to combine.
2. **Serve**: Add ice and top with whipped cream if desired. Enjoy the rich mocha and almond flavors with a refreshing cold brew base.

Cold Brew Coffee with Coconut Water

Ingredients:

- 1 cup cold brew coffee
- 1/2 cup coconut water
- Ice
  Instructions:
1. **Combine the Drinks**: In a glass, mix cold brew coffee and coconut water. Stir well.
2. **Serve**: Add ice and stir again to enjoy a refreshing, hydrating coffee drink with a tropical twist.

Cold Brew Coffee Mojito

Ingredients:

- 1 cup cold brew coffee
- 10-12 fresh mint leaves
- 1 tbsp lime juice
- 1-2 tsp sugar (or to taste)
- Ice
- Club soda

Instructions:

1. **Muddle the Mint**: In a glass, muddle mint leaves with lime juice and sugar.
2. **Mix the Drink**: Add cold brew coffee, stir well, and fill the glass with ice.
3. **Top with Soda**: Pour in club soda and stir gently. Garnish with extra mint leaves for a refreshing twist on the classic mojito.

Iced Nitro Cold Brew Float

Ingredients:

- 1 cup nitro cold brew coffee
- 1 scoop vanilla ice cream
- Chocolate syrup (optional)
  Instructions:
1. **Prepare the Float**: In a tall glass, add a scoop of vanilla ice cream.
2. **Add the Nitro Cold Brew**: Pour the nitro cold brew coffee over the ice cream.
3. **Serve**: Drizzle with chocolate syrup if desired. Enjoy a fizzy, creamy coffee float.

Cold Brew Coffee with Cardamom

Ingredients:

- 1 cup cold brew coffee
- 1/4 tsp ground cardamom
- 1 tbsp honey or sugar (optional)
- Ice
  Instructions:
1. **Mix the Ingredients**: In a glass, combine cold brew coffee, cardamom, and honey or sugar (if desired). Stir well.
2. **Serve**: Add ice and stir again to enjoy a warm-spiced, aromatic cold brew.

Honey Lavender Cold Brew

Ingredients:

- 1 cup cold brew coffee
- 1 tbsp honey
- 1/2 tsp dried lavender flowers
- Ice

Instructions:

1. **Infuse the Lavender**: Steep dried lavender in hot water for a few minutes, then strain and cool.
2. **Mix the Drink**: In a glass, combine cold brew coffee, honey, and lavender infusion. Stir well.
3. **Serve**: Add ice and enjoy a fragrant, floral coffee drink.

Cold Brew Ginger Coffee

Ingredients:

- 1 cup cold brew coffee
- 1-2 tbsp fresh ginger syrup (or grated ginger)
- Ice
- Lemon slice (optional)
  Instructions:
1. **Mix the Ingredients**: In a glass, combine cold brew coffee and ginger syrup. Stir well.
2. **Serve**: Add ice and garnish with a slice of lemon for a zesty, spicy coffee experience.

Cold Brew Frappe

Ingredients:

- 1 cup cold brew coffee
- 1/2 cup milk (or dairy-free alternative)
- 1/2 cup ice
- 1 tbsp sugar or sweetener (optional)
- Whipped cream (optional)

Instructions:

1. **Blend**: In a blender, combine cold brew coffee, milk, ice, and sweetener. Blend until smooth and frothy.
2. **Serve**: Pour into a glass and top with whipped cream if desired. Enjoy a creamy, chilled coffee treat.

Matcha Cold Brew Latte

Ingredients:

- 1 cup cold brew coffee
- 1 tsp matcha powder
- 1/2 cup milk (or dairy-free alternative)
- 1-2 tsp honey or sweetener (optional)
- Ice

Instructions:

1. **Prepare Matcha**: In a small bowl, whisk matcha powder with a little warm water to dissolve.
2. **Mix the Drink**: In a glass, combine cold brew coffee, matcha mixture, and milk. Stir well.
3. **Serve**: Add ice and sweeten with honey or your choice of sweetener. Enjoy a layered, earthy coffee latte with a green tea twist.

Cold Brew with Chocolate Syrup

Ingredients:

- 1 cup cold brew coffee
- 2 tbsp chocolate syrup
- Ice
- Whipped cream (optional)

Instructions:

1. **Mix the Ingredients**: In a glass, combine cold brew coffee and chocolate syrup. Stir well to combine.
2. **Serve**: Add ice and top with whipped cream for a sweet, chocolaty coffee experience.

Strawberry Cold Brew Iced Coffee

Ingredients:

- 1 cup cold brew coffee
- 1/4 cup fresh strawberry puree (or strawberry syrup)
- 1 tbsp sugar (optional)
- Ice
- Milk (optional)

Instructions:

1. **Prepare Strawberry Puree**: Blend fresh strawberries until smooth, or use pre-made strawberry syrup.
2. **Mix the Drink**: In a glass, combine cold brew coffee, strawberry puree, and sweetener. Stir well.
3. **Serve**: Add ice and milk if desired for a creamy finish. Enjoy a refreshing fruity twist on your cold brew.

Spiced Pumpkin Cold Brew Latte

Ingredients:

- 1 cup cold brew coffee
- 1/4 cup pumpkin puree
- 1/2 tsp pumpkin spice
- 1-2 tsp brown sugar or sweetener (optional)
- 1/2 cup milk (or dairy-free alternative)
- Ice

Instructions:

1. **Prepare Pumpkin Mixture**: In a small saucepan, combine pumpkin puree, pumpkin spice, and sweetener. Heat gently until smooth.
2. **Mix the Drink**: In a glass, combine cold brew coffee, pumpkin mixture, and milk. Stir well.
3. **Serve**: Add ice and enjoy a fall-inspired, spiced cold brew latte.

Cold Brew Coffee Milkshake

Ingredients:

- 1 cup cold brew coffee
- 1/2 cup vanilla ice cream
- 1/4 cup milk (or dairy-free alternative)
- Whipped cream (optional)

Instructions:

1. **Blend the Milkshake**: In a blender, combine cold brew coffee, vanilla ice cream, and milk. Blend until smooth and creamy.
2. **Serve**: Pour into a glass and top with whipped cream for a decadent cold brew milkshake.

Cold Brew Coffee with Coconut Milk and Spice

Ingredients:

- 1 cup cold brew coffee
- 1/2 cup coconut milk
- 1/4 tsp cinnamon
- 1/4 tsp nutmeg
- Ice

Instructions:

1. **Mix the Ingredients**: In a glass, combine cold brew coffee, coconut milk, cinnamon, and nutmeg. Stir well.
2. **Serve**: Add ice and enjoy a creamy, spiced cold brew with a tropical coconut flavor.

Cold Brew Cherry Blossom Latte

Ingredients:

- 1 cup cold brew coffee
- 1 tbsp cherry blossom syrup (or cherry syrup)
- 1/2 cup milk (or dairy-free alternative)
- Ice

    Instructions:

1. **Mix the Drink**: In a glass, combine cold brew coffee and cherry blossom syrup. Stir well.
2. **Serve**: Add milk and ice. Stir to combine for a floral and sweet cherry-inspired cold brew latte.

Cold Brew Coffee with Vanilla Syrup

Ingredients:

- 1 cup cold brew coffee
- 2 tbsp vanilla syrup
- Ice
- Milk or cream (optional)

Instructions:

1. **Mix the Drink**: In a glass, combine cold brew coffee and vanilla syrup. Stir well.
2. **Serve**: Add ice and milk or cream if desired for a smooth, sweet, and fragrant coffee experience.

Cold Brew Coffee Tonic

Ingredients:

- 1 cup cold brew coffee
- 1/2 cup tonic water
- Ice
- Lemon slice (optional)

Instructions:

1. **Prepare the Drink**: In a glass, combine cold brew coffee and tonic water.
2. **Serve**: Add ice and garnish with a lemon slice for a refreshing and slightly bitter coffee tonic.

Lemon Ginger Cold Brew Coffee

Ingredients:

- 1 cup cold brew coffee
- 1 tbsp lemon juice
- 1/2 tsp ginger syrup (or grated fresh ginger)
- Ice

  Instructions:

1. **Mix the Drink**: In a glass, combine cold brew coffee, lemon juice, and ginger syrup. Stir well.
2. **Serve**: Add ice and enjoy the refreshing, zesty combination of lemon and ginger with your cold brew coffee.

Cold Brew Coconut Iced Coffee

Ingredients:

- 1 cup cold brew coffee
- 1/2 cup coconut milk
- 1-2 tsp sweetener (optional)
- Ice

Instructions:

1. **Mix the Drink**: In a glass, combine cold brew coffee and coconut milk. Stir well.
2. **Serve**: Add ice and sweeten with sugar or your preferred sweetener for a tropical twist on your cold brew coffee.

Cherry Cold Brew Coffee

Ingredients:

- 1 cup cold brew coffee
- 2 tbsp cherry syrup (or fresh cherry puree)
- Ice
- Milk or cream (optional)
Instructions:
1. **Mix the Drink**: In a glass, combine cold brew coffee and cherry syrup or puree. Stir well.
2. **Serve**: Add ice and milk or cream for a sweet and fruity cold brew coffee experience.

Cold Brew Caramel Macchiato

Ingredients:

- 1 cup cold brew coffee
- 2 tbsp caramel syrup
- 1/4 cup milk or cream
- Ice

   Instructions:

1. **Prepare the Drink**: In a glass, add ice, then pour in the cold brew coffee and caramel syrup.
2. **Top Off**: Gently pour in the milk or cream, creating a layered effect. Stir before drinking to combine the flavors of caramel and coffee.

Cold Brew Coffee with Coconut Cream and Cocoa

Ingredients:

- 1 cup cold brew coffee
- 2 tbsp coconut cream
- 1 tsp cocoa powder
- 1 tsp sweetener (optional)
- Ice

Instructions:

1. **Mix the Drink**: In a shaker, combine cold brew coffee, coconut cream, cocoa powder, and sweetener (if using).
2. **Serve**: Shake well and pour over ice for a rich, creamy, and chocolatey cold brew coffee.

Tropical Cold Brew Coffee

Ingredients:

- 1 cup cold brew coffee
- 1/4 cup pineapple juice
- 1/4 cup coconut milk
- Ice

Instructions:

1. **Mix the Drink**: In a glass, combine cold brew coffee, pineapple juice, and coconut milk. Stir until smooth.
2. **Serve**: Add ice for a tropical twist on your usual cold brew coffee.

Cold Brew Coffee with Orange Zest

Ingredients:

- 1 cup cold brew coffee
- 1 tsp orange zest
- 1 tbsp orange juice
- Ice

    Instructions:

1. **Mix the Drink**: In a glass, combine cold brew coffee, orange zest, and orange juice. Stir well to combine the citrusy notes with the coffee.
2. **Serve**: Add ice for a refreshing, aromatic cold brew with a citrus kick.

Cold Brew Coffee with Almond Syrup

Ingredients:

- 1 cup cold brew coffee
- 1-2 tbsp almond syrup (or almond extract)
- Ice
- Milk or cream (optional)

Instructions:

1. **Mix the Drink:** In a glass, combine cold brew coffee and almond syrup. Stir well.
2. **Serve:** Add ice and optional milk or cream for a nutty, slightly sweet cold brew experience.

www.ingramcontent.com/pod-product-compliance
Lightning Source LLC
LaVergne TN
LVHW081331060526
838201LV00055B/2585